BENEFITS OF GOING THROUGH

THE GREAT TRIBULATION

Studio of Books LLC
5900 Balcones Drive Suite 100
Austin, Texas 78731
www.studioofbooks.org
Hotline: (254) 800-1183

Ordering Information:
Special discounts are available on quantity purchases by corporations, associations, and others. For details, contact the publisher at the address above.

Printed in the United States of America.

ISBN-13: Softcover   978-1-968491-82-6
          eBook   978-1-968491-83-3

BENEFITS OF GOING THROUGH

THE GREAT TRIBULATION

ELWOOD TROST

CONTENTS

PREFACE

The Bible reveals the benefits of going through trials and tribulations. Therefore, it would make sense that if we are called to endure the Great Tribulation that there be even greater benefits involved. I cover some benefits in this book that we will receive by going through the Great Tribulation.

Most of us have an aversion of going through tribulations and would rather escape them, but if we know the truth of why God allows us to be tested, it will encourage us to change our minds or at least have a better attitude towards the Great Tribulation because it has been given a bad wrap in many cases and some Christians won't even read the Book of Revelation.

As I see God's perspective on tribulation, and how it changes us and how it deepens our relationship with Him; it gives me another reason to see the Great Tribulation in a better light.

The book of Revelation is the revelation of Our Lord and Savior Jesus Christ (Revelation 1:1). At a wedding, it is how the groom reveals Himself so we can see his character. In this wedding the groom is the center of attention, so why shouldn't we, **as the bride,** want to be there and see the revelation of Jesus Christ?

When we see what God is accomplishing by sending His judgments, which are redemptive, and that many are repenting and coming into the Kingdom of God during the Great Tribulation, it should encourage us to be part of this great harvest of souls. the Great Tribulation is God's harvest time and Jesus tells us to pray for laborers to be sent into the harvest:

> *The Lord now chose seventy-two other disciples and sent them ahead in pairs to all the towns and places he planned to visit. These were his instructions to them: "The harvest is great, but the workers are few. So, pray to the Lord who is in charge of the harvest; ask him to send more workers into his fields (Luke 10.1-2).*

The parable of the wheat and tares:

> *Jesus replied, "The Son of Man is the farmer who plants the good seed. The field is the world, and the good seed represents the people of the Kingdom. The weeds are the people who belong to the evil one. The enemy who planted the weeds among the wheat is the devil. **The harvest is the end of the world**, and the harvesters are the angels. "Just as the weeds are sorted out and burned in the fire, so it will be at the end of the world. The Son of Man will send his angels, and they will remove from his Kingdom everything that causes sin and all who do evil. And the angels will throw them into the fiery furnace, where there will be weeping and gnashing of teeth. Then the righteous will shine like the sun in their Father's Kingdom. Anyone with ears to hear should listen and understand! (Matthew 13: 37-43).*

We see that **harvest is at the end of the world** when the good seed is caught up and gathered together to be with the Lord at the same time the weeds are gathered and thrown into the fiery furnace. Heaven is coming to earth not the other way around. The reason we are caught up and gathered to be with Jesus is so we can be gathered instantly from one end of heaven to the other, and another reason is we cannot go through the center of the earth. When we meet the Lord in the air, we escort Him back to earth to help Him rule and reign during His millennial reign.

A type and shadow of this is the triumphant entry of Jesus on a donkey to die for our sins, but this time He will be riding a white horse (symbol of pure power) to rule and reign the earth.

On a closer examination of Scripture, we see there is not a rapture but a resurrection at the second coming. Jesus doesn't come back twice but only once which makes the Post-Trib rapture the most correct view of the second coming.

In chapter eleven of Hebrews, which is referred to as the faith chapter and records the heroes of the faith, we read they went through their fiery trials gladly and victoriously knowing that they would experience a better resurrection:

> *It was by faith that Moses, when he grew up, refused to be called the son of Pharaoh's daughter. He chose to share the oppression of God's people instead of enjoying the fleeting pleasures of sin. He thought it was better to suffer for the sake of Christ than to own the treasures of Egypt, for he was looking ahead to his great reward (Hebrews 11:24-26).*

Those going through the Great Tribulation will receive great benefits and rewards they would never trade, and they will have eternity to enjoy them.

Therefore, we do not lose heart. Even though our outward man is perishing, yet the inward man is being renewed day by day. For our light affliction, which is but for a moment, is working for us a far more exceeding and eternal weight of glory, while we do not look at the things which are seen, but at the things which are not seen. For the things which are seen are temporary, but the things which are not seen are eternal (2 Corinthians 2:16-18 NKJV).

Father, help us get our minds on the eternal benefits of going through the Great Tribulation and meet it in faith and not in fear, in Jesus' Name, Amen!

INTRODUCTION

Many are concerned about the timing of the rapture, and we should be because one fourth of the Bible is about the second coming of Jesus Christ. But I would like to put that aside for now and talk about the benefits of being here during the Great Tribulation if we happen to find ourselves in it.

It will be the worst time in human history according to Jesus (Matthew 24:21).

Therefore, those who are here will need a powerful prayer life and a close relationship with the Lord. They will need to know the Word of God and be in fellowship with likeminded believers who are encouraging one another.

If we are called to go through it, Jesus will be the fourth man in the fire, and His faithful followers will be able to encourage us and we will be able to encourage them!

> *Let us hold tightly without wavering to the hope we affirm, for God can be trusted to keep his promise. Let us think of ways to motivate one another to acts of love and good works. And let us not neglect our meeting together, as some people do, but encourage one another, especially now that the day of his return is drawing near (Hebrews 10:23-25).*

The battle we will be in is not to be responding in fear but in faith. The False Prophet will be performing signs and wonders, and many will be deceived and give allegiance to the Antichrist by taking the "Mark of the Beast."

We will need to keep our hearts soft because Jesus tells us that many will fall away and betray one another under the persecution of the Antichrist because their hearts will grow cold.

> *"Then you will be arrested, persecuted, and killed. You will be hated all over the world because you are my followers. And many will turn away from me and betray and hate each other. And many false prophets will appear and will deceive many people. Sin will be rampant everywhere, and the love of many will grow cold. But the one who endures to the end will be saved. And the Good News about the Kingdom will be preached throughout the whole world, so that all nations will hear it; and then the end will come. The day is coming when you will see what Daniel the prophet spoke about—the sacrilegious object that causes desecration standing in the Holy Place." (Reader, pay attention!) Then those in Judea must flee to the hills"* (Matthew 24:9-16).

Jesus puts this persecution at the midpoint of Daniel's 70th Week. This is when the Antichrist breaks the peace treaty, invades Israel, sets up the "abomination of desolation," and sits in the temple claiming to be God. This is when the Great Tribulation begins and lasts for 3½ years until Jesus returns.

It will be important to know that God loves us and has not forsaken us even if it may look like that at times. It will be important for us to understand why we are being tested and what God is accomplishing in us.

I will be covering some benefits I see from the Scriptures for those who are called to go through the Great Tribulation.

> *Be careful that you do not refuse to listen to the One who is speaking. For if the people of Israel did not escape when they refused to listen to Moses, the earthly messenger, we will certainly not escape if we reject the One who speaks to us from heaven! When God spoke from Mount Sinai his voice shook the earth, but now he makes another promise: "Once again I will shake not only the earth but the heavens also." This means that all of creation will be shaken and removed, so that only unshakable things will remain. Since we are receiving a Kingdom that is unshakable, let us be thankful and please God by worshiping him with holy fear and awe. For our God is a devouring fire (Hebrews 12:25-29).*

God is and will be shaking everything that is built on sand and the only thing that will remain is His Kingdom and those "who endure to the end."

If you haven't found your ministry yet, be encouraged because some of the greatest ministries are still in the future. "The first will be last and the last will be first."

Father, help us meet the Great Tribulation which is at the door with the right attitude and help us realize the great honor of being here if we are called to go through it, in Jesus' Name, Amen!

CHAPTER ONE

First Benefit
More Power and Authority

One benefit of being here during the Great Tribulation is that believers in Yeshua (Jesus) will see an increase in power.

> *Then I heard a loud voice shouting across the heavens, "It has come at last—salvation and power and the Kingdom of our God, and the authority of his Christ. For the accuser of our brothers and sisters has been thrown down to earth—the one who accuses them before our God day and night (Revelation 12:10).*

The context of chapter twelve of Revelation is the Great Tribulation which is the last 3½ years of this age. Satan is casted out of heaven and possesses the Antichrist. The last 3½ years is referred to twice in this chapter; in verse six as 1260 days (Hebrew month being 30 days); and in verse fourteen as time, times, and half a time.

Power and authority will be restored to the followers of Jesus during this time. Signs and wonders will be following the preaching of the Word. This does not mean you cannot walk in the power and authority of Jesus now, but when the dark gets darker the light gets brighter.

We will do the greater works that Jesus told us we would do (John 14:12). Many believers will be casting out demons, raising the dead, and healing the sick, but at the same time being persecuted by the Antichrist. Because of our increase in power and authority many will come to faith in Jesus, and we will see a great harvest of souls come into the Kingdom of God.

> *After this I saw a vast crowd, too great to count, from every nation and tribe and people and language, standing in front of the throne and before the Lamb. They were clothed in white robes and held palm branches in their hands. And they were shouting with a great roar, "Salvation comes from our God who sits on the throne and from the Lamb!" Then one of the twenty-four elders asked me, "Who are these who are clothed in white? Where did they come from?" And I said to him, "Sir, you are the one who knows. "Then he said to me, "These are the ones who died in the great tribulation. They have washed their robes in the blood of the Lamb and made them white. (Revelation 7:9-10;13-14).*

Therefore, benefit number one is more power and authority returning to believers in Jesus Christ.

Father, I thank You for the power and authority You will be giving us that will bring many into Your kingdom, in Jesus' Name, Amen!

CHAPTER TWO

Second Benefit
Defeating the Antichrist

Looking at the next two verses in chapter twelve of Revelation and remembering the context of this chapter is the Great Tribulation, we understand that we will have the privilege of defeating the Antichrist, who is Satan in the flesh.

> *And they have defeated him (the Antichrist) by the blood of the Lamb and by their testimony. And they did not love their lives so much that they were afraid to die. Therefore, rejoice, O heavens! And you who live in the heavens, rejoice! But terror will come on the earth and the sea, for the Satan has come down to you in great anger, knowing that he has little time (3 ½ years) (Revelation 12:11-12).*

When devil is thrown out of heaven, he possesses the Antichrist, and the Tribulation Saints defeat him by the blood of the Lamb, their testimony, and by laying down their lives. They will defeat the Antichrist the same way Jesus defeated Satan by going to the cross.

It doesn't appear like a victory but when Jesus returns at the end of the Great Tribulation, he will avenge them. He will bring justice by raising The Tribulation Saints from the dead and destroying the Antichrist. Our hope is in resurrection, not a rapture.

Apostle Paul confirms this:

> *In his justice he will pay back those who persecute you. And God will provide rest for you who are being persecuted and also for us when the Lord Jesus appears from heaven. He will come with his mighty angels, in flaming fire, bringing judgment on those who don't know God and on those who refuse to obey the Good News of our Lord Jesus. They will be punished with eternal destruction, forever separated from the Lord and from his glorious power. When he comes on that day, he will receive glory from his holy people—praise from all who believe. And this includes you, for you believed what we told you about him (2 Thessalonians 1:6-10).*

Satan knows his time is short. So, he goes around raising havoc which is recorded in Isaiah:

> *In that wonderful day when the Lord gives his people rest from sorrow and fear, from slavery and chains, you will taunt the king of Babylon. You will say, "The mighty man has been destroyed. Yes, your insolence is ended. For the Lord has crushed your wicked power and broken your evil rule. You struck the people with endless blows of rage and held the nations in your angry grip with unrelenting tyranny. But finally, the earth is at rest and quiet. Now it can sing again! Even the trees of the forest—the cypress*

trees and the cedars of Lebanon—sing out this joyous
song: 'Since you have been cut down, no one will come
now to cut us down!'" (Isaiah 14:3-8).

Notice the Great Tribulation is what sets us free from the world's
systems that have us in bondage today.

Isaiah continues:

How you are fallen from heaven, O shining star, son of
the morning! You have been thrown down to the earth,
you who destroyed the nations of the world. For you said
to yourself, 'I will ascend to heaven and set my throne
above God's stars. I will preside on the mountain of the
gods far away in the north. I will climb to the highest
heavens and be like the Most High.' Instead, you will be
brought down to the place of the dead, down to its lowest
depths. Everyone there will stare at you and ask, 'Can this
be the one who shook the earth and made the kingdoms
of the world tremble? Is this the one who destroyed the
world and made it into a wasteland? Is this the king who
demolished the world's greatest cities and had no mercy on
his prisoners?' (Isaiah 14:12-17).

The Antichrist accepts the offer from Satan to rule the nations
that Jesus refused, and Jesus will become the rightful ruler over the
earth when He returns. During the millennial reign of Christ, the
cities will be repaired and restored.

Isaiah gives a glimpse into the millennial reign of Christ when
we are with Him in Israel:

To all who mourn in Israel, he will give a crown of beauty for ashes, a joyous blessing instead of mourning, festive praise instead of despair. In their righteousness, they will be like great oaks that the Lord has planted for his own glory. They will rebuild the ancient ruins, repairing cities destroyed long ago. They will revive them, though they have been deserted for many generations. Foreigners will be your servants. They will feed your flocks and plow your fields and tend your vineyards. You will be called priests of the Lord, ministers of our God. You will feed on the treasures of the nations and boast in their riches. Instead of shame and dishonor, you will enjoy a double share of honor. You will possess a double portion of prosperity in your land, and everlasting joy will be yours (Isaiah 61:3-7).

So, benefit number two is the Tribulation Saints will have the honor of destroying the Antichrist. I believe these will be the ones who will experience double honor during eternity.

Father, thank You for Your Word that shows us the benefits we will receive if we are called to endure the Great Tribulation, in Jesus' Name, Amen!

CHAPTER THREE

Third Benefit
Ambassadors of Truth

From the book of Daniel, we can get some insight on what ministry will look like during the Great Tribulation.

Then at the appointed time he (the Antichrist) will once again invade the south, but this time the result will be different. For warships from western coastlands will scare him off, and he will withdraw and return home. But he will vent his anger against the people of the holy covenant and reward those who forsake the covenant. "His army will take over the Temple fortress, pollute the sanctuary, put a stop to the daily sacrifices, and set up the sacrilegious object that causes desecration. He will flatter and win over those who have violated the covenant. But the people who know their God will be strong and will resist him. "Wise leaders will give instruction to many, but these teachers will die by fire and sword, or they will be jailed and robbed" During these persecutions, little help

*will arrive, and many who join them will not be sincere.
And some of the wise will fall victim to persecution. In
this way, they will be refined and cleansed and made pure
until the time of the end, for the appointed time is still; to
come" (Daniel 11: 29-35).*

Daniel 9:27 reveals that the sacrifices are stopped by the
Antichrist halfway through the last seven years. Therefore, it appears
this invasion takes place at that time and then the Great Tribulation
begins.

Jesus confirms the timing of this invasion:

*"The day is coming when you will see what Daniel the
prophet spoke about—the sacrilegious object that causes
desecration standing in the Holy Place." (Reader, pay
attention!) "Then those in Judea must flee to the hills
(Matthew 24:15-16).*

The timing of this invasion of Israel is also recorded in the gospel of Luke:

*"And when you see Jerusalem surrounded by armies,
then you will know that the time of its destruction has
arrived. Then those in Judea must flee to the hills. Those
in Jerusalem must get out, and those out in the country
should not return to the city" (Luke 21:20-21).*

The good news is that the Antichrist does not appear to control
the whole world because ships from the Western coastlands oppose
him. (Maybe the United States). The Antichrist will be in control

of the Middle East and the nations that are surrounding Israel that want her destruction.

Also, later in this chapter eleven of Daniel we see some other nations he doesn't have control over.

> But news from the east and north shall trouble him (Daniel 11:44).

It is important when we are interpreting eschatology is that we understand it is mainly about the Middle East, and not the West.

My speculation is that the Antichrist is a Muslim and more than likely from Turkey. Erdogan, the leader of Turkey, is restoring the Caliphate which is made up of the ten nations that surround Israel. He hates Israel and is on Hamas' side. I am not saying Erdogan is the Antichrist, but he could be laying the groundwork for him.

Does persecution bring revival or does revival bring persecu-tion? They seem to go together. It is interesting the countries where Christians are being persecuted like China, Iran, North Korea, and some Africa nations are the fastest growing churches today.

The third benefit of being here during the Great Tribulation will be those who know their God will be strong and have the power to resist the Antichrist and defeat him, and in a world of deception and false prophets, they will be able to give instructions to many and lead them into the truth and prevent them from taking the "Mark of the Beast." All those who take the mark will experience the wrath of God.

Father, thank You for having led us out of deception and given us the truth of what You are doing in these last days so that we can be ambassadors of Your truth and help many come out of darkness into Your light, in Jesus' Name, Amen!

CHAPTER FOUR

Fourth Benefit
Being Purified

I am not claiming you must go through the Great Tribulation to be purified because all who come to Jesus are purified by the fiery trials and tribulations and no one is exempt, but I am looking at some benefits you will receive if you are called to go through it that would encourage you and help you endure to the end.

The Prophet Daniel reveals that the persecution of the Antichrist will refine those who go through it:

> *During these persecutions, little help will arrive, and many who join them will not be sincere. And some of the wise will fall victim to persecution. In this way, they will be refined and cleansed and made pure until the time of the end, for the appointed time is still to come (Daniel 11:34-35).*

If we have ever wondered, why God just doesn't take us home when we first come to Jesus, one reason is He must clean us up first, so we don't pollute heaven.

Let's look at a portion of Scripture that implies the bride has made herself ready by going through the Great Tribulation:

> *Then I heard again what sounded like the shout of a vast crowd or the roar of mighty ocean waves or the crash of loud thunder: "Praise the Lord! For the Lord our God, the Almighty, reigns. Let us be glad and rejoice and let us give honor to him. For the time has come for the wedding feast of the Lamb, and his bride has prepared herself. She has been given the finest of pure white linen to wear." For the fine linen represents the good deeds of God's holy people. And the angel said to me, "Write this: Blessed are those who are invited to the wedding feast of the Lamb." And he added, "These are true words that come from God"* (Revelation 19:6-9).

If we put the verses from Daniel together with these from chapter nineteen of the book of Revelation, we see that bride has made herself ready. So, does this mean that to be part of the bride you must go through the Great Tribulation? I don't know but it looks that way.

The wedding feast is on the earth after Jesus returns and not in heaven. We will enjoy the marriage supper of the lamb on earth eating real food and drinking real wine. Heaven is coming to earth. Thy kingdom come, Thy will be done on earth as it is in heaven.

The Hebrew children in the fiery furnace are a type and foreshadow of those who will not bow to the Antichrist and worship him. Jesus was in the fire with them, and He will be here to protect those who go through the fire of the Great Tribulation.

Those who think all they must do is say a prayer and then they will be whisked to heaven in their present condition have been deceived. It is true when they accept Jesus, they are justified, but the Bible says they must also be sanctified, which means to be made holy and that takes time and work:

> *Therefore, my beloved, as you have always obeyed, not as in my presence only, but now much more in my absence, work out your own salvation with fear and trembling; for it is God who works in you both to will and to do for His good pleasure (Philippians 2:12-13 NKJV).*

Psalm 46 was written for a time as the Great Tribulation:

> *God is our refuge and strength, always ready to help in times of trouble. So, we will not fear when earthquakes come and the mountains crumble into the sea. Let the oceans roar and foam. Let the mountains tremble as the waters surge! A river brings joy to the city of our God, the sacred home of the Most High. God dwells in that city; it cannot be destroyed. From the very break of day, God will protect it. The nations are in chaos, and their kingdoms crumble! God's voice thunders, and the earth melts! The Lord of Heaven's Armies is here among us; the God of Israel is our fortress. Interlude Come, see the glorious works of the Lord: See how he brings destruction upon the world. He causes wars to end throughout the earth. He breaks the bow and snaps the spear; he burns the shields with fire. "Be still and know that I am God! I will be*

honored by every nation. I will be honored throughout the world." The Lord of Heaven's Armies is here among us; the God of Israel is our fortress (Psalm 46:1-11).

Be still, in the Greek, means stop doing what you are doing and spend some time with God in prayer:

Let the whole world bless our God and loudly sing his praises. Our lives are in his hands, and he keeps our feet from stumbling. You have tested us, O God; you have purified us like silver. You captured us in your net and laid the burden of slavery on our backs. Then you put a leader over us. We went through fire and flood, but you brought us to a place of great abundance (Psalm 66:8-12).

And:

When you go through deep waters, I will be with you. When you go through rivers of difficulty, you will not drown. When you walk through the fire of oppression, you will not be burned up; the flames will not consume you (Isaiah 43:2).

Notice that God says when you go through the fire, not when you escape it.

Therefore, the fourth benefit of going through the Great Tribulation is for our refining that will make us a people ready to meet our God.

Father, thank You for Your protection as we go through the fire of the Great Tribulation that will purify us and get us ready to meet Jesus in the air, in Jesus' Name, Amen!

CHAPTER FIVE

Fifth Benefit
Sharing in His Glory

"At that time Michael, the archangel who stands guard over your nation, will arise. Then there will be a time of anguish greater than any since nations first came into existence. But at that time every one of your people whose name is written in the book will be rescued. Many of those whose bodies lie dead and buried will rise up, some to everlasting life and some to shame and everlasting disgrace. Those who are wise will shine as bright as the sky, and those who lead many to righteousness will shine like the stars forever" (Daniel 12:1-3).

Daniel's revelation puts those who are wise and lead many to righteousness into the context of the Great Tribulation, and they are the ones that are promised the glory of shining like the stars forever. This momentary hardship will produce an eternity of glory for those who are fortunate to be here during the Great Tribulation.

Apostle Paul tells us that we must share in Christ's suffering if we are going to share in His glory:

> *So, you have not received a spirit that makes you fearful slaves. Instead, you received God's Spirit when he adopted you as his own children. Now we call him, "Abba, Father." For his Spirit joins with our spirit to affirm that we are God's children. And since we are his children, we are his heirs. In fact, together with Christ we are heirs of God's glory. But if we are to share his glory, we must also share his suffering (Romans 8:15-17).*

Jesus tells us many will fall away during the Great Tribulation because of the persecution of the Antichrist that begins at the midpoint of Daniel's 70th Week.

My question is why do so many fall away halfway through the last seven years if we have been raptured?

> *"Then you will be arrested, persecuted, and killed. You will be hated all over the world because you are my followers. And many will turn away from me and betray and hate each other. And many false prophets will appear and will deceive many people. Sin will be rampant everywhere, and the love of many will grow cold. But the one who endures to the end will be saved. And the Good News about the Kingdom will be preached throughout the whole world, so that all nations will hear it; and then the end will come. "The day is coming when you will see what Daniel the prophet spoke about—the sacrilegious object that causes desecration standing in the Holy Place."*

(Reader, pay attention!) "Then those in Judea must flee to the hills." (Matthew 24:9-16).

One of the reasons that the love of many will grow cold is because of the lawlessness in the world, but we do not have to lose our love if we have a close relationship with the God of love. God will give us the courage to endure to the end. This is why we are exhorted to keep a soft heart during times of testing and learn to forgive those who are persecuting us and bless them. So, we don't have to be one who falls away from the faith.

God has promised us that we would not be tested beyond what we can handle:

> *The temptations in your life are no different from what others experience. And God is faithful. He will not allow the temptation to be more than you can stand. When you are tempted, he will show you a way out so that you can endure (1 Corinthians 10:13).*

We can get through the days ahead as we pray, read His Word, and fellowship with like-minded believers. The more tribulation we go through the more rewards, benefits, and treasures we will have forever.

Apostle Paul says this about suffering:

> *I once thought these things were valuable, but now I consider them worthless because of what Christ has done. Yes, everything else is worthless when compared with the infinite value of knowing Christ Jesus my Lord. For his sake I have discarded everything else, counting it all as garbage, so that I could gain Christ and become one with*

him. I no longer count on my own righteousness through obeying the law; rather, I become righteous through faith in Christ. For God's way of making us right with himself depends on faith. I want to know Christ and experience the mighty power that raised him from the dead. I want to suffer with him, sharing in his death, so that one way or another I will experience the resurrection from the dead! (Philippians 3:7-11).

Therefore, the modern teachings that are being taught by many fellowships today that leave out suffering and an escape from the Great Tribulation are false teachings.

The fifth benefit of going through the Great Tribulation is it qualifies us to share in God's glory.

Father, help us teach the truth and not twist Scripture to support what tickles our ears. Help us understand how You use suffering to make us candidates to share in Your glory. in Jesus' Name, Amen!

CHAPTER SIX

Sixth Benefit
Reigning with Christ

Then I saw thrones, and the people sitting on them had been given the authority to judge. And I saw the souls of those who had been beheaded for their testimony about Jesus and for proclaiming the word of God. They had not worshiped the beast or his statue, nor accepted his mark on their foreheads or their hands. They all came to life again, and they reigned with Christ for a thousand years. This is the first resurrection. (The rest of the dead did not come back to life until the thousand years had ended.) Blessed and holy are those who share in the first resurrection. For them the second death holds no power, but they will be priests of God and of Christ and will reign with him a thousand years (Revelation 20:4-6).

These who do *not* take the "Mark of the Beast" will be resurrected at the first resurrection and sit on thrones ruling and reigning with Christ.

Every believer in Jesus Christ is ruling and reigning through our prayers today, but these Tribulation Saints are given authority to judge and rule for the millennial reign of Christ. These earned this authority because when they were tested by fire and proved themselves faithful.

Jesus said:

> *"God blesses you when people mock you and persecute you and lie about you and say all sorts of evil things against you because you are my followers. Be happy about it! Be very glad! For a great reward awaits you in heaven. And remember, the ancient prophets were persecuted in the same way" (Matthew 5:11-12).*

The fifth seal of Revelation chapter six is about martyrdom which is referring to the persecution by the Antichrist that happens during the Great Tribulation:

> *When the Lamb broke the fifth seal, I saw under the altar the souls of all who had been martyred for the word of God and for being faithful in their testimony. They shouted to the Lord and said, "O Sovereign Lord, holy and true, how long before you judge the people who belong to this world and avenge our blood for what they have done to us?" Then a white robe was given to each of them. And they were told to rest a little longer until the full number of their brothers and sisters—their fellow servants of Jesus who were to be martyred—had joined them (Revelation 6:9-11).*

The Great Tribulation will be an opportunity to grow in love with one another and for believers to put up some treasure in heaven. The good news is God takes the soul and spirit of those being martyred just before they are killed, so they don't feel any pain.

The Great Tribulation is our training for reigning. God will burn away the pride in us and replace it with humility:

> *Is there any encouragement from belonging to Christ? Any comfort from his love? Any fellowship together in the Spirit? Are your hearts tender and compassionate? Then make me truly happy by agreeing wholeheartedly with each other, loving one another, and working together with one mind and purpose. Don't be selfish; don't try to impress others. Be humble, thinking of others as better than yourselves. Don't look out only for your own interests, but take an interest in others, too. You must have the same attitude that Christ Jesus had. Though he was God, he did not think of equality with God as something to cling to. Instead, he gave up his divine privileges; he took the humble position of a slave and was born as a human being. When he appeared in human form, he humbled himself in obedience to God and died a criminal's death on a cross. Therefore, God elevated him to the place of highest honor and gave him the name above all other names, that at the name of Jesus every knee should bow, in heaven and on earth and under the earth, and every tongue declare that Jesus Christ is Lord, to the glory of God the Father (Philippians 2:1-11).*

The sixth benefit I see from Scripture is becoming a candidate that is qualified to rule and reign with Christ.

Father, give us the grace to stand firm during our time of testing and become candidates to rule and reign with You, in Jesus' Name, Amen!

CHAPTER SEVEN

Seventh Benefit
Growing in the Lord

Dear brothers and sisters, when troubles of any kind come your way, consider it an opportunity for great joy. For you know that when your faith is tested, your endurance has a chance to grow. So let it grow, for when your endurance is fully developed, you will be perfect and complete, needing nothing (James 1:2-4).

My question is what should our attitude be about going through tribulation when the Bible teaches us to consider it an opportunity for great joy? We can have joy if we know the truth that they are making us more like Jesus. The tribulations we will be experiencing during the Great Tribulation will bring us closer to perfection by causing us to grow in our endurance, and in character which strengthens our hope of salvation, which will increase our ability to love.

Therefore, since we have been made right in God's sight by faith, we have peace with God because of what Jesus Christ our Lord has done for us. Because of our faith, Christ has brought us into this place of undeserved privilege where we now stand, and we confidently and joyfully look forward to sharing God's glory. We can rejoice, too, when we run into problems and trials, for we know that they help us develop endurance. And endurance develops strength of character, and character strengthens our confident hope of salvation. And this hope will not lead to disappointment. For we know how dearly God loves us, because he has given us the Holy Spirit to fill our hearts with his love (Romans 5:1-5).

Hope is important to survive hard times. We can trust God's Word because He never breaks a promise:

Hope deferred makes the heart sick, but a dream fulfilled is a tree of life (Proverbs 13:12).

When we encounter trouble, and we will, we are required to make a choice to either walk in the Spirit or in our flesh (our lower nature). If we choose to trust the Lord and walk in the Spirit, we will receive the joy of the Lord.

But the Holy Spirit produces this kind of fruit in our lives: love, joy, peace, patience, kindness, goodness, faithfulness, gentleness, and self-control. There is no law against these things! Those who belong to Christ Jesus have nailed the passions and desires of their sinful nature to his cross and crucified them there (Galatians 5:22-24).

If we walk in the Spirit during hard times we will grow in these virtues, but If we choose to walk in the flesh, we will see what is wrong with everything and end up depressed, and God has given us a freewill to choose.

Let's begin giving thanks for everything and step out of our depression. We don't need medication for our depression, we need a closer walk with Jesus.

> *Always be joyful. Never stop praying. Be thankful in all circumstances, for this is God's will for you who belong to Christ Jesus (1 Thessalonians 5:16-18).*

The Lord revealed to me by giving thanks we receive the mind of Christ instead of the mind of the enemy.

I was in an emergency room one day getting stitches between two of my fingers and the moment I began to give thanks, I noticed that my thinking changed from being negative to becoming positive. Instead of seeing how bad this cut was, I began to see that there were no cut tendons and how I wasn't out in a jungle miles from a doctor and was being taken care of within minutes after the accident. Therefore, I began to learn that giving thanks in all things is a powerful spiritual weapon:

> *Shout with joy to the Lord, all the earth! Worship the Lord with gladness. Come before him, singing with joy. Acknowledge that the Lord is God! He made us, and we are his. We are his people, the sheep of his pasture. Enter his gates with thanksgiving; go into his courts with praise. Give thanks to him and praise his name. For the Lord is good. His unfailing love continues forever, and his faithfulness continues to each generation (Psalm 100).*

Our troubles change us from being self-centered to being Christ centered. Any of us who have walked with the Lord for some time realize our flesh doesn't die easily, but the Great Tribulation will help us get it done.

I love Psalm 34:

I will praise the Lord at all times. I will constantly speak his praises. I will boast only in the Lord; let all who are helpless take heart. Come, let us tell of the Lord's greatness; let us exalt his name together. I prayed to the Lord, and he answered me. He freed me from all my fears. Those who look to him for help will be radiant with joy; no shadow of shame will darken their faces. In my desperation I prayed, and the Lord listened; he saved me from all my troubles. For the angel of the Lord is a guard; he surrounds and defends all who fear him. Taste and see that the Lord is good. Oh, the joys of those who take refuge in him! Fear the Lord, you his godly people, for those who fear him will have all they need. Even strong young lions sometimes go hungry, but those who trust in the Lord will lack no good thing. Come, my children, and listen to me, and I will teach you to fear the Lord. Does anyone want to live a life that is long and prosperous? Then keep your tongue from speaking evil and your lips from telling lies! Turn away from evil and do good. Search for peace, and work to maintain it. The eyes of the Lord watch over those who do right; his ears are open to their cries for help. But the Lord turns his face against those who do evil; he will erase their memory from the earth. The Lord hears his people when they call to him for help. He rescues them from all their troubles. The Lord is close to the broken hearted; he rescues those whose spirits are crushed. The righteous person faces many troubles, but the Lord comes to the rescue each time. For the Lord protects the bones of the righteous; not one of them is broken! Calamity will surely destroy the wicked, and those who hate the righteous will be punished. But the Lord will redeem those who serve him. No one who takes refuge in him will be condemned (Psalm 34).

We are to seek peace and work for it. Listening to the truth and rejecting the lies of the enemy and taking every thought captive will be important if we are going to remain in peace:

We are human, but we don't wage war as humans do. We use God's mighty weapons, not worldly weapons, to knock down the strongholds of human reasoning and to destroy false arguments. We destroy every proud obstacle that keeps people from knowing God. We capture their rebellious thoughts and teach them to obey Christ (2 Corinthians 10:3-5).

Same Scripture from the New King James Version is:

For though we walk in the flesh, we do not war according to the flesh. For the weapons of our warfare are not carnal but mighty in God for pulling down strongholds, casting down arguments and every high thing that exalts itself against the knowledge of God, bringing every thought into captivity to the obedience of Christ (2 Corinthians 10:3-5 NKJV).

If your heart is broken, be encouraged the Lord is close, and He recues those who spirits are crushed. The righteous person faces many troubles, but the Lord comes to the rescue every time. I have walked with the Lord for fifty years and I have found this to be true.

Therefore, the seventh benefit of going thought the Great Tribulation is growing in the Lord.

Father, give us the bigger picture of what You are doing through our difficulties we face, and give us the ability to rejoice and understand they are necessary for growing in the Lord, in Jesus' Name, Amen!

CHAPTER EIGHT

Eighth Benefit
Restoration of the Fear of the Lord

It doesn't take a prophet to realize the church is out of balance towards grace and lacks the fear of the Lord. The meaning of fear of the Lord in Scripture ranges from the awesome respect of believers to a fearful dread for the unbeliever. The Bible has many promises for those who fear the Lord. When we see the power of God released through the Seals, Trumpets, Bowl Judgments of Revelation, the fear (awesome respect) of the Lord will return to the church and dreadful fear to the world, and many will come into the Kingdom of God because of these judgments.

Let's look at some of the promises of those who fear the Lord:

> *The Lord merely spoke, and the heavens were created.*
> *He breathed the word, and all the stars were born. He*
> *assigned the sea its boundaries and locked the oceans in*
> *vast reservoirs. Let the whole world **fear the Lord and***
> ***let everyone stand in awe of him**. For when he spoke,*
> *the world began! It appeared at his command. The Lord*

*frustrates the plans of the nations and thwarts all their schemes. But the Lord's plans stand firm forever; his intentions can never be shaken. What joy for the nation whose God is the Lord, whose people he has chosen as his inheritance. **But the Lord watches over those who fear him**, those who rely on his unfailing love. **He rescues them from death and keeps them alive in times of famine.** We put our hope in the Lord. He is our help and our shield. In him our hearts rejoice, for we trust in his holy name. Let your unfailing love surround us, Lord, for our hope is in you alone (Psalm 33:6-12; 18-22).*

God promises to protect those who fear Him and provide for them in times of famine. During the Great Tribulation, no one will be able to buy or sell unless they take the "Mark of the Beast" and if they do, they will experience the wrath of God. But those who fear the Lord will **not** have to live in fear because we have a promise from God that He will provide for us.

Jesus supernaturally fed 5,000 men plus the women, and children with five loaves and two fish (Matthew 14:16-21). Another time He fed 4,000 men plus women and children with seven loaves and a few fish (Matthew 15:32-38).

Also, there is a story in the Old Testament of how God provided for a widow who feared the Lord and obeyed Him:

Then the Lord said to Elijah, "Go and live in the village of Zarephath, near the city of Sidon. I have instructed a widow there to feed you." So, he went to Zarephath. As he arrived at the gates of the village, he saw a widow gathering sticks, and he asked her, "Would you please bring me a little water in a cup?" As she was going to get it, he called to her, "Bring me a bite of bread, too." But she said, "I swear by the Lord your God that I don't have a single piece of bread in the house. And I have only a handful of flour left in the jar and a little cooking oil in the bottom of the jug. I was just gathering a few sticks to cook this last meal, and then my son and I will die." But Elijah said to her, "Don't be afraid! Go ahead and do just what you've said but make a little bread for me first. Then use what's left to prepare a meal for yourself and your son. For this is what the Lord, the God of Israel, says: There will always be flour and olive oil left in your containers until the time when the Lord sends rain, and the crops grow again!" So, she did as Elijah said, and she and Elijah and her family continued to eat for many days. There was always enough flour and olive oil left in the containers, just as the Lord had promised through Elijah (1 Kings 17:8-16).

If we listen to and obey the Holy Spirit during the Great Tribulation, we will have plenty to eat. This is a good reason to work on hearing the voice of God today.

Notice, it is our weaknesses that God can manifest His glory. God promises provision for His children, and He never breaks a promise. It will be a testimony when we cannot buy or sell, and others see how God is providing for us.

What shall we say about such wonderful things as these? If God is for us, who can ever be against us? Since he did not spare even his own Son but gave him up for us all, won't he also give us everything else? Who dares accuse us whom God has chosen for his own? No one—for God himself has given us right standing with himself. Who then will condemn us? No one—for Christ Jesus died for us and was raised to life for us, and he is sitting in the place of honor at God's right hand, pleading for us. Can anything ever separate us from Christ's love? Does it mean he no longer loves us if we have trouble or calamity, or are persecuted, or hungry, or destitute, or in danger, or threatened with death? (As the Scriptures say, "For your sake we are killed every day; we are being slaughtered like sheep.") No, despite all these things, overwhelming victory is ours through Christ, who loved us. And I am convinced that nothing can ever separate us from God's love. Neither death nor life, neither angels nor demons, neither our fears for today nor our worries about tomorrow—not even the powers of hell can separate us from God's love. No power in the sky above or in the earth below—indeed, nothing in all creation will ever be able to separate us from the love of God that is revealed in Christ Jesus our Lord (Romans 8:31-39).

No worries for the believer who fears the Lord and puts his trust in Him.

But the love of the Lord remains forever with those who fear him. His salvation extends to the children's children (Psalm 103:17).

This promise is for our children and grandchildren too!

Fear of the Lord is the foundation of wisdom. Knowledge of the Holy One results in good judgment. Wisdom will multiply your days and add years to your life (Proverbs 9:10-11).

The eighth benefit I mention is the Great Tribulation will restore the fear of the Lord to His people. We are to fear the Lord and not people and what they can do to us: Let's begin to fear the Lord and repent of our fear of man.

The Lord is on my side; I will not fear. What can man do to me? (Psalm 118:6).

Father, thank You for Your promises and how You never break a promise. Help us learn to fear You and not man, in Jesus' Name, Amen!

CHAPTER NINE

Ninth Benefit
Transformed into the Image of Jesus

One of the greatest benefits of all is God will use the Great Tribulation to conform us into the image of Jesus.

> *Likewise the Spirit also helps in our weaknesses. For we do not know what we should pray for as we ought, but the Spirit Himself makes intercession for us with groanings which cannot be uttered. Now He who searches the hearts knows what the mind of the Spirit is, because He makes intercession for the saints according to the will of God. And we know that all things work together for good to those who love God, to those who are the called according to His purpose. For whom He foreknew, He also predestined to be conformed to the image of His Son, that He might be the firstborn among many brethren (Romans 8:26-29 NKJV).*

The Bible says Jesus learned obedience by the things He suffered.

> *While Jesus was here on earth, he offered prayers and pleadings, with a loud cry and tears, to the one who could rescue him from death. And God heard his prayers because of his deep reverence for God. Even though Jesus was God's Son, he learned obedience from the things he suffered. In this way, God qualified him as a perfect High Priest, and he became the source of eternal salvation for all those who obey him. And God designated him to be a High Priest in the order of Melchizedek (Hebrews 5:7-10).*

Jesus, who was without sin learned obedience by the things he suffered. Where does that put us? Could this be one reason that God allows us to go through the Great Tribulation?

If we think we can be whisked away in a Pre-Trib Rapture while we are in our present condition, we are deceived and don't understand God's purpose for the Great Tribulation.

Let's start believing the Bible over the teachings that tickle our ears because we are in the closing years of this age and the Great Tribulation will be here sooner than many believe. It is time to get on the same page with God and start bringing in the harvest of souls that will populate heaven.

Many believers will fall away when persecution comes according to the Bible, and I believe it is because they believe in Jesus but haven't developed a personal relationship with Him by making Him Lord of their lives. They believe but they continue to live for themselves and not for God.

Religion will not get us through what is coming and only a personal relationship with the living God will give us the grace to endure to the end.

I hope this book will encourage those who find themselves going through trials and tribulations because no one escapes them.

Let me close this chapter with this Psalm that is given to us for such a time as the Great Tribulation:

> *Those who live in the shelter of the Most High will find rest in the shadow of the Almighty. This I declare about the Lord: He alone is my refuge, my place of safety; he is my God, and I trust him. For he will rescue you from every trap and protect you from deadly disease. He will cover you with his feathers. He will shelter you with his wings. His faithful promises are your armor and protection. Do not be afraid of the terrors of the night, nor the arrow that flies in the day. Do not dread the disease that stalks in darkness, nor the disaster that strikes at midday. Though a thousand fall at your side, though ten thousand are dying around you, these evils will not touch you. Just open your eyes and see how the wicked are punished. If you make the Lord your refuge, if you make the Most High your shelter, no evil will conquer you; no plague will come near your home. For he will order his angels to protect you wherever you go. They will hold you up with their hands, so you won't even hurt your foot on a stone. You will trample upon lions and cobras; you will crush fierce lions and serpents under your feet! The Lord says, "I will rescue those who love me. I will protect those who trust in my name. When they call on me, I will answer; I will be with them in trouble. I will rescue and honor them. I will reward them with a long life and give them my salvation (Psalm 91).*

The ninth benefit of going through the Great Tribulation is to be conformed to the image of Jesus.

Father, help us believe the truth and give us the grace to make You the Lord of our life and go through the hard times that will conform us to be like Jesus, in Jesus' Name, Amen!

CHAPTER TEN

God's Harvest Time
Tenth benefit is helping to
bring in the harvest

As I shared in the Preface, God's judgments are redemptive and bring in a great harvest of souls. When we can show the unbelievers of how God judgments were recorded in the Bible many will begin to believe.

Jesus prophesied that earthquakes would be one of the signs His second coming. When we had an earthquake in California in 1970, it got my attention. I wondered who this Jesus was who had such knowledge and could predict things 2,000 years in advance. So, I got a bible and in the gospel of John, I read that one needed to be born-again (speaking of our spirit) and asked for that and to my surprise it happened.

Then I learned that why Jesus could know in advance these things was because He was God in the flesh.

It will be evangelistic to see the judgments of Revelation being released just like they are written about in the book of Revelation. We read in Revelation chapter seven that there are so many saved during the Great Tribulation that they cannot be counted (Revelation 7:9-17).

Jesus never prayed we would escape the Great Tribulation, but He did pray for our protection:

> *I'm not asking you to take them out of the world, but to keep them safe from the evil one (the Antichrist). They do not belong to this world any more than I do. Make them holy by your truth; teach them your word, which is truth. Just as you sent me into the world, I am sending them into the world. And I give myself as a holy sacrifice for them so they can be made holy by your truth. "I am praying not only for these disciples but also for all who will ever believe in me through their message. I pray that they will all be one, just as you and I are one—as you are in me, Father, and I am in you. And may they be in us so that the world will believe you sent me. "I have given them the glory you gave me, so they may be one as we are one. I am in them, and you are in me. May they experience such perfect unity that the world will know that you sent me and that you love them as much as you love me (John 17:15-23).*

Jesus prayed for unity and protection for His church and not for our escape. You don't send your field workers home during harvest time, but all are to be involved in bringing it in.

I see some verses in Revelation chapter where God has prepared a place in the wilderness for the woman, who is the upgraded Jacob that includes all believers in Yeshua. God has also provided food for us because we cannot buy or sell during the Great Tribulation.

If we keep chapter twelve in context, the male child she gives birth too could be the 144,000 that are sealed to go through the wrath of God. These will rule and reign with Jesus. How can they be caught up to heaven and be here at the same time? It is because that describes all believers in (Yeshua) Jesus because we are all sitting with Him in heaven, and we are still here on earth at the same time.

(72 x 2,000, for 2,000 years, equals 144,000)

> *The Lord now chose seventy-two other disciples and sent them ahead in pairs to all the towns and places he planned to visit. These were his instructions to them: "The harvest is great, but the workers are few. So, pray to the Lord who is in charge of the harvest; ask him to send more workers into his fields (Luke 10:1-2).*

Could this chapter ten in Luke be a type and shadow of the harvesters of end of the age and do the instructions in this chapter apply to this time? If it does, let's look at what their marching orders will look like:

> *Now go and remember that I am sending you out as lambs among wolves. Don't take any money with you, nor a traveler's bag, nor an extra pair of sandals. And don't stop greeting anyone on the road. "Whenever you enter someone's home, first say, 'May God's peace be on this house.' If those who live there are peaceful, the bless- ing will stand; if they are not, the blessing will return to you. Don't move around from home to home. Stay in one place, eating and drinking what they provide. Don't hes- itate to accept hospitality, because those who work deserve their pay. "If you enter a town and it welcomes you, eat*

whatever is set before you. Heal the sick, and tell them, 'The Kingdom of God is near you now.' But if a town refuses to welcome you, go out into its streets and say, 'We wipe even the dust of your town from our feet to show that we have abandoned you to your fate. And know this— the Kingdom of God is near!' I assure you; even wicked Sodom will be better off than such a town on judgment day (Luke 10:3-12).

If they go into a town and start healing the sick, soon crowds will be at the doors hearing the gospel and the mission field will be coming to them and this could explain the great harvest is a short period of time.

The tenth benefit of being part of the Great Tribulation is we would have the honor of being part of God's harvest time.

Father, we thank You that You have not given up on Your creation and never will and that You have revealed to those who will listen to what You have planned for the near future, in Jesus' Name, Amen!

CONCLUSION

I have written this book to help us to see the Great Tribulation in a more positive way:

> *I beseech you therefore, brethren, by the mercies of God, that you present your bodies a living sacrifice, holy, acceptable to God, which is your reasonable service. And do not be conformed to this world, but be transformed by the renewing of your mind, that you may prove what is that good and acceptable and perfect will of God (Romans 12:1-2 NKJV).*

I have shared some benefits of going through the Great Tribulation to help you renew your mind about it. God will be using the Great Tribulation to bring His kingdom to earth and put Jesus on the throne and to restore all things.

The believers who are here at that time will have an increase in power and authority. They will have the privilege of defeating the Antichrist and enjoying that memory forever. They will be able to bring the truth to many while the world is under the deception of the Antichrist and False Prophet. They will be refined in the fire and come out looking like Jesus by growing in love and endurance, and they will be the harvesters of the end of the age.

The Great Tribulation is also training for reigning *(Revelation 20:4-6).*

The feasts of the Lord found in Leviticus chapter 23 are prophetic. The spring feasts were fulfilled by Jesus to the day and hour at His first coming.

Fifty days later, Pentecost was fulfilled when God poured His Spirit out on the church.

The fall feasts are yet to be fulfilled and are a rehearsal of the second coming.

Jesus returns on the Feast of Trumpets and leads a military campaign against the Antichrist and his army. Nine days later, the Day of Atonement happens which is Armageddon, and five days after that the Feast of Tabernacles begins which the marriage supper of the Lamb.

If Jesus returns on the Feast of Trumpets, that will mean the last seven years (Daniel's 70th Week) should begin on the Feast of Trumpets, seven years earlier.

Therefore, I believe this will be the next prophecy to be fulfilled, so let's be watching for it:

> *The ruler will make a treaty with the people for a period of one set of seven (seven years), but after half this time, he will put an end to the sacrifices and offerings. And as a climax to all his terrible deeds, he will set up a sacrilegious object that causes desecration, until the fate decreed for this defiler is finally poured out on him (Daniel 9:27).*

I will close by saying that the book of Revelation is the revelation of Jesus, and we should want to be here to see it, no matter how difficult of a time it might be:

"You can enter God's Kingdom only through the narrow gate. The highway to hell is broad, and its gate is wide for the many who choose that way. But the gateway to life is very narrow and the road is difficult, and only a few ever find it" (Matthew 7:13-14).

And:

Because we have these promises, dear friends, let us cleanse ourselves from everything that can defile our body or spirit. And let us work toward complete holiness because we fear God (2 Corinthians 7:1).

Father, thank You for the hope we have for a good future with You. Give us the grace to get through the Gret Tribulation. I pray that everyone who reads this book would be encouraged and have the strength to keep the faith and endure to the end, In Jesus' Name, Amen!

www.ingramcontent.com/pod-product-compliance
Lightning Source LLC
Chambersburg PA
CBHW051243120626
46547CB00014B/1781